The Ancient Parish of St. Budeaux

Marshall Ware

Delivering Milk in St. Budeaux
The very popular Mrs. Cann is seen here delivering milk in Coldrenick Street sometime during the First World War. She is assisted by her daughter, Mrs. Doidge, serving milk not with bottles but by measuring out quantities from the large churns seen on the cart.

This version of the book is virtually as originally published, presenting the work of Marshall Ware. There are now additional pages at the back providing information about the publisher, Arthur L Clamp.

The republishing project is being managed by Arthur's grandson, Steven Gibson. We aim to find all the research that he was involved in publishing, preserving it for the next generation as part of 'The Clamp Collection'.

THE ANCIENT PARISH OF ST. BUDEAUX

ONE OF the good things to be set in the balance sheet of present day English villages is the growing practice of producing local histories before scenes disappear; this particularly applies to St. Budeaux where conditions are changing so rapidly with the impact of the new *Tamar Bridge* road that *Arthur Clamp* has invited me to record some of the changes that are taking place. He has planned the reproduction of the pictorial records for publication with his usual skill and enthusiasm.

We have no knowledge of the actual date of the building of the first church in this parish; all we know for certain is that in the year 1331 the Church of St. Budoc was placed under the care of the Priory of Plympton. The present church was built in 1563, and according to the *Kalendar* in Exeter Cathedral archives, St. Budoc's Day is 8th December, and for many years was celebrated as a Day of Thanksgiving in the parish. As the population grew ten places of worship have been provided for the people of the parish: some of these are now independent parish churches, and some are used as parish halls, while others have now ceased to exist. The most important person buried in the church was Lady Drake on 2nd January, 1582, and an archaeologist with a sensitive metal detector has recently located a lead coffin near the Gorges Memorial which may be Lady Drake's.

Among the many famous people who have worshipped in the church are Sir Francis Drake, Captain Sir Thomas Byard, Lieut. John Chard, V.C. (Rorke's Drift fame), Lieut-Comdr. Malleston V.C. (Gallipoli Campaign) and Admiral Sir Peter Richards, K.C.B., Lord Commissioner of the Admiralty, who at one time commanded the *Cornwallis* and *Hibernia*. St. Peter's Mission Chapel (blitzed in 1941) was dedicated to perpetuate his memory on 23rd September, 1885. Unfortunately Miss Anne Slemon who was born at Bull Point on the 25th October, 1882, died last year at the age of 99, but we still have Mr. Ernest Parkhouse aged, 98, who we hope will live to be a centenarian.

Apart from the parish registers, which date back to 1538, we are fortunate in having our ancient history recorded by R. N. Worth and Crispin Gill. We are also grateful to H. M. Evans (1842-1930) for *St. Budeaux, Its Manors and First Church*, W. C. Menheneott for *Memories of St. Budeaux in 1870*, and George H. Ivory, a civil engineer, for *The St. Budeaux of 1892*, who states, "There were no resident doctors and no health services. Nightsoil was buried in the back garden. Water was hand-pumped from the well in each garden. There was no gas, nor electric light, no health insurance, no unemployed, no buses, no trams, no automobiles, no aeroplanes, no wireless and no cinema. The only two great inventions in the countryside in those days were the railways and the telegraph—when they were available." It must be remembered at that time we were in Plympton R.D.C. and the Tavistock Parliamentary Division. In fact my father's birth certificate dated 2nd March, 1872, states, "Born in the District of Tavistock in the Counties of Devon and Cornwall." When Devonport absorbed a large part of the parish in 1898, they provided a gas, water supply and sewage system, which together with the opening of the London and South Western railway station in 1890, helped the parish building expansion.

After working in Cornwall, Devon and Somerset, I was transferred in 1934, to work in my home town where I renewed acquaintance with Mr. and Mrs. J. F. Donne (nee King). She was born at Butshead Mill (now Budshead Mill), daughter of William King (1832-1912) and she remembered her grandfather, Walter King (1805-1869) and her grandmother, Emmeline Bonney, whose family have farmed at Agaton and Kings Tamerton for nearly 200 years; Jacob Bonney's name is inscribed on the church bell cast in 1888. Among the exciting family records carefully preserved by the Donne family are the St. Budeaux Foundation School samplers dated 1840 and earlier, the Cookson family bible, weighing 28 lbs. bound in leather by J. Drew, 8 New Street, Dock, and the fabulous 1750 Prayer Book used for worship by the Bonneys in St. Budeaux Church and correspondence with the Rev. B. J. S. Vallack (1832-1875) who was the vicar before the burial vault of Lady Mary Drake was filled in. Mrs. Donne showed me the site in the north east aisle where Lady Drake is reputed to have been buried. She said the church bells were rung when Francis Drake married Mary Newman said to have been born at Agaton Farm, a member of the important Newman family. From the marriage registers we find that her eldest sister, Maude, married Lyon Worthie (Lord of the Manor of East Whitleigh) on 25th November, 1552. There is also the parish correspondence from Sir Ralph Newman and of course local tradition is valuable evidence in matters of this kind. She considered the story taken from a historical romatic novel, written by a woman author called *Pleasant Hours*, in 1895, stating that Mary Newman's father was a humble fisherman is completely untrue.

These are but a few of the facets that conjure up colourful pictures of the bygone days; yet they have not receded too far into the past for there are still persons alive who remember them.

Marshall Ware,
800 Wolseley Road,
St. Budeaux,
Plymouth, Devon
March, 1983

Royal Albert Bridge Sailing Club

Founder members of the sailing club, one attired for the occasion, are grouped for the photographer on St. Budeaux Quay sometime in 1932. The name of the club had to be changed to Tamar River Sailing Club by order of the Secretary of State because the club did not hold a charter.

The Bowling Green

A nostalgic view of the bowling green, Northcott's bakery (now the Co-op super market), St. Budeaux Library, housed in a wooden hut, four Cavell Terrace shops and St. Boniface Church and Hall.

A Fiftieth Anniversary

The smiles of this group record the fiftieth anniversary of the St. Boniface Church Mothers' Union with the Rev. and Mrs. P. J. White in attendance. Mesdames Chappell, Bullard, Tedder, Collett, Harris, Sanderson, Chown, Williams, Screech, Deacon, Heywood, Pearce, Meadows and Roach form the group.

The Barne Barton Boys, 1950

Smiling faces and plenty of enthusiasm tell here of a successful season of speedway cycling once popular in the area. The *Eagles* had a tremendous following and competed against the Ernesettle *Boars*. Note the old prefabs in the background.

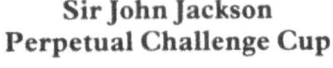

Cycling Champion in 1912

Cycle racing has been very well supported in this area for many years and many local lads have gained awards for their achievements. Fred Johns sits proudly on his bike with his displays gained for his club and himself.

Sir John Jackson Perpetual Challenge Cup

Mr. Horrill of Kings Tamerton was the winner of this cup in 1900, competed for by members of the local cycling clubs. The very ornamented large cup was a cherished prize named after Sir John Jackson, M.P., who built the Keyham Dockyard extension and the Weston Mill Estate for his workers.

Miss Ida Worth's Class 5

Her class poses for the camera here at Victoria Road School. Among those identified are the names of Rhodes, Hockey, Hutchings, Angle, Holland, Horsham, Stevens, Bowen, Hammett, Richards, Daymond, Smith, Thomas, Dustan, Pearse, Hancock, Maker, Miss Worth, Oldridge, Strike, Woodall, Banbury, Mitchell, Adams, Wilcocks, Glanville, Hillam, Holmes, Selley and Luscombe.

Victoria Road School

In the back row, fourth from left, is Miss Ivy Ferris (now Mrs. Rosevear) who served in the W.R.E.N.S., taught in Victoria Road School and is now a Ward Councillor. The group photograph will recall many memories of this school with its single tree in the tiled playground and, no doubt, many people will recognise themselves as children in those now distant pre-war days.

Marriage Entry, St. Budeaux Church, 1569

These entries are reproduced from the composite marriage registers of the church showing (second line down) the marriage record of Francis Drake to Mary Newman on 4th July, 1569.

The Arms of Drake

These were granted to Drake in 1518 by Queen Elizabeth I for his services to the country. The shield is symbolising the two hemispheres with the world encompassed. The ship at the top is guided around the globe by the Divine hand of Providence, *Auxilio Divino*. Below is the open visor indicating his rank. The lower inscription, Great Achievements From Small Beginnings, *Sic Parvis Magna*, summarises Drake's life style and ambitions (a photograph of the arms is in the parish church).

Burial Entry, St. Budeaux Church, 1582

These few lines from the composite burial register show the entry for the burial of Lady Mary Drake (second line down), wife of Sir Francis Drake which took place on 25th January, 1582.

First Railway Station Master

In 1890 Mr. Edmund Tolley was appointed the first L. and S.W. Railway station master for St. Budeaux. A well loved character he will be remembered for occasionally holding up a train in the station for latecomers!

Captain Charlie Daymond

He is seen here with his family outside 8 Morris Park Terrace and of the boys, only Sidney (looking at the family cat) is still living and his sister, Florence, a retired headteacher resident in St. Budeaux. Captain Daymond owned three barges and employed eleven men to transport bricks from the Southdown works to Camel's Head Quay and Tripp's Wharf then to Victoria Road and Camel's Head Schools. The brass plate next door indicates the Rate Office and Registrar of Births and Deaths. It was also the Parish Police Station controlled by Sergeant Wallis.

Rev. J. T. Trelawny Ross
Earl Compton and the Trelawny family were the main St. Budeaux landowners. The Rev. Trelawney Ross with his wife and family are here outside Ham House.

A Letter of Thanks
This is part of a letter of thanks which the Rev. Trelawny Ross sent to those who gave flowers at his wife's funeral in 1935. His wife was very well respected and took an active part in local affairs.

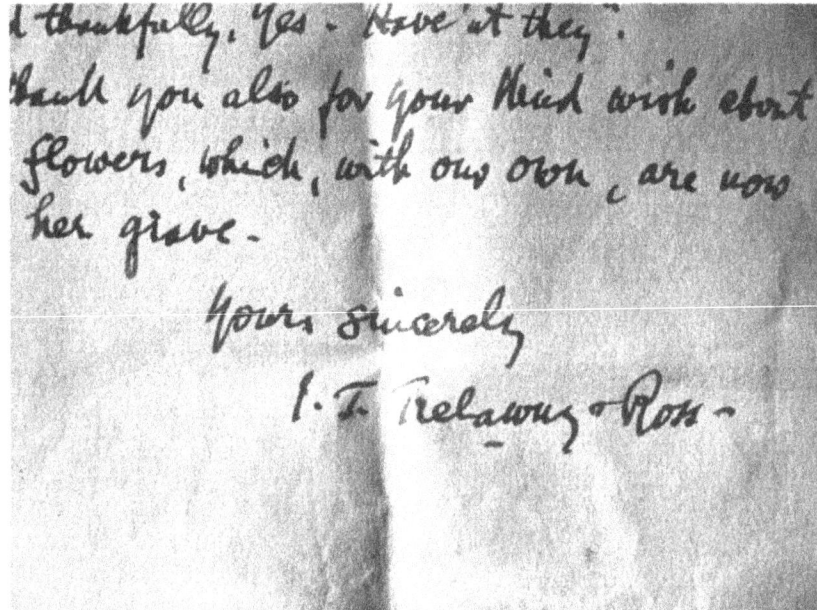

1898 Marriage Ceremony
The marriage of James F. Donne, builder, and Mary King (Budshead Mill) outside Waverley Villa (Tamar Terrace) united two very old local families.

These two photographs were taken in about 1875 by H. Montagu Evans and show the building in ruins.

Budshead Mansion

In 1280 Peter de Sancte Antonio became Prior of Plympton and in 1273 was Superior of Budshead and probably the small body monks there were responsible for the services of the church. Later it would seem that the services were conducted by a priest who lived at St. Andrew's Prysten House in Plymouth. This gave rise to local opinion that Budshead was a monastery. The late Fred Baker, together with older residents, always called it by that name.

Copy of part of Lord Ashburton's rent book.

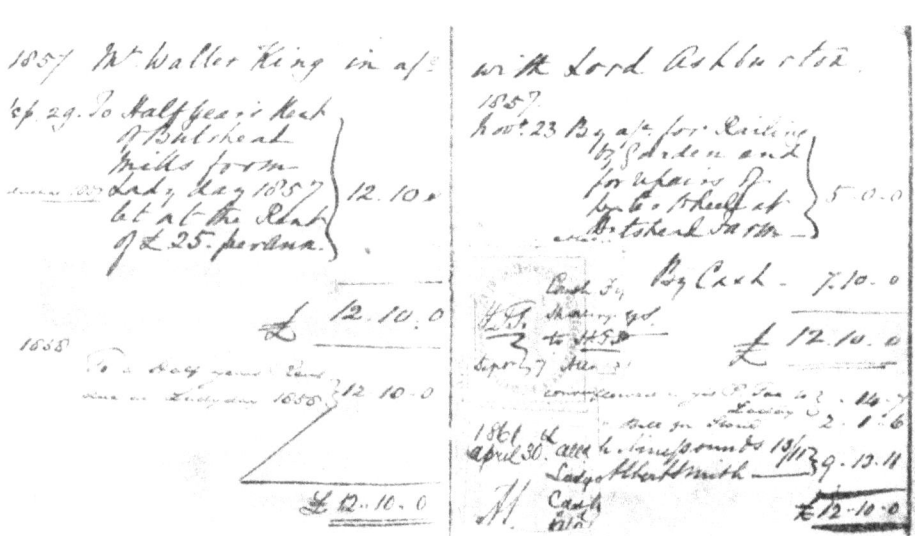

Mr. King was the tenant of Budshead Mills and Earl Compton (later to become Lord Northampton) inherited the property.

The Marchioness of Northampton

Mr. Ernest Parkhouse

Born in 1884 he is one of our oldest and most respected senior citizens and is seen here outside his father's cycle works pumping up a tyre. This workshop employing two apprentices was typical of the many small enterprises in the area. He had a distinguished career in H.M. Dockyard and was awarded the B.E.M. and the 25 and 50 year T. and G. W. Union medals.

Interior of Methodist Chapel

This photograph was taken in 1893 and will recall many connections with the old chapel by local people. The building is now used by the British Legion. The Parkhouse family are long members of this local cause.

Mr. Ben Petherick

He is seen here outside his Weston Mill overshot water wheel which is covered with ice following a very cold spell. Note the family resemblance to his grandson, Edward Petherick, who was a very popular Victoria Road school teacher. Affectionately known as "Slab Petherick", the reason for this is not known.

Rev. T. A. Hancock, M.A.

This popular vicar served the parish from 1929 to 1941 and took a keen interest in local history writing two booklets, *St. Budeaux Church: Its Documents and Treasures* and *The Bells of St. Budeaux.* He fostered good relations with the Methodists and Baptists.

Mrs. Trelawny Ross

A great local stalwart who undertook a lot of charitable work in the parish. She died in 1935 at the age of 81 years. Many local people will quickly recall the days when she was one of the local leaders who many people looked up to and respected.

Mr. Fred Baker

We were all very sorry when Mr. Baker died early in 1982 at the age of 84 years, after spending a lifetime on Agaton Farm which dates back to 1313. He was the last of our yeoman farmers in this area having succeeded his father, W. T. Baker, to the property. He was a regular rider with the St. Budeaux foxhounds and eighty members attended a meet at Yelverton on Saturday 4th November, 1933.

Trelawny Hotel

Courage Breweries has given the hotel a face lift and placed the Trelawny coat of arms in a prominent position outside the building. A wine store occupies the entrances to the former coaching stables.

Wooden Camel's Head

This large and beautifully carved figure was a feature of the interior of *Camel's Head Inn* for many years but was removed when Courage sold out to Bass who changed the name of the house to *The Submarine*.

Old St. Budeaux Inn

This was the title before it had its present name. Lord Graves, Lord of the manor of Agaton, was the owner of the then *Church Inn* in 1798 and the landlord, Francis Martin, changed the name to *St. Bude Inn* in 1828. In 1862 the War Department bought it with stables and sold it to James Algar in 1914. The Octagan Brewery acquired it in 1939; it is now owned by Courage.

The Trelawny Hotel

General John Jago Trelawny, owner of the Barne Estate, sold the site of 6,272 feet to Joseph Stribling for £157 who, with a loan of £4,300, erected the Trelawny Hotel in 1895 with two bars, a bar parlour, club room, coach house, outbuildings, stables and yards; Mr. Stribling died in 1897. The Plymouth Octagon Brewery acquired the premises and gave a ten year lease to Harry Hearn. He was followed by a long line of popular landlords, the outstanding one being Bill Howett, seen seated in a dark suit with his customers before the departure of the Bank holiday wagonette outing. This was the first of the St. Budeaux buildings to be lit by electricity. Maurice Wilson, the Plymouth Albion and Devon rugby stalwart, remembers using the old engine changing room and iron bath when he played for St. Budeaux Rugby Club. Courage have recently given the hotel a face lift and placed the Trelawny coat of arms inside and outside of the premises.

The Parish Builders

In about 1900 Mr. J. F. Donne combined forces with Tozer and Allen to build Lynher Terrace; in 1902, 2 Lynher Terrace was occupied by the Baptist Pastor the Rev. Henry Smart. The old methods of working required more men than today which gave a source of income for many local tradesmen working in the locality.

The Parish Builders

This photograph dates from 1900 and shows J. T. Donne's building yard off Vicarage Road (now Normandy Way). His father, James Donne, built a number of houses in this area from 1890 onwards and the Donne family owned over thirty at one time. Note the large carriage for carrying timber with a long horse shaft on the left.

Church Workers at Weston Mill

Mr. George Ellery is at the head of the horse with a team of volunteers digging the foundation for St. Phillip's Church Hall on land off Churchway. This was given by Mr. Cleave. The vicar, the Rev. J. T. T. Browne, appointed in 1930, can be seen with clerical collar, plus cap, holding a spade and supported by Messrs. Foster, Carpenter, May and Cleave.

Seal of the Prince of Wales

Some of the old Saltash Passage property deeds had the ancient seal of the Prince of Wales, Duke of Cornwall, on them. This interesting link came from the time when St. Budeaux was part of the Duchy of Cornwall's estate.

Ernesettle Road Houses

The bottom Ernesettle Road buildings have been demolished to make way for the new Tamar Bridge road and a former resident, Mr. Hatherley, will be sad to see his old home gone.

Drake's Drum

This famous drum is now kept in Buckland Abbey. Drake took it with him on his expeditions and over the years it has been used as a symbol in times of war.

St. Budeaux Freemasons

Freemasonry had widespread support from the local business community and members of various local churches. Some of the headstones in the churchyard bear masonic insignia showing the deceased's connection with this movement. It was decided to to form a new lodge so the Queen Victoria Lodge. No. 2655 came into being on 13th February, 1897. It used the Trelawny Hotel lodge room until the Masonic Hall was completed in 1899.

Share Certificate of 1897

Eight Craft Lodges now use this as their focal point for social activities and the sum of £1,250 was soon raised by a public issue of shares. One certificate is shown here giving details of that now far off event in the Jubilee year of the reign of Queen Victoria whose name it commemorates.

Masonic Ritual Mug

These two large illustrations show both sides of this cup which is still kept in the possession of a local masonic family. The eight-line poem makes interesting reading and sets some guidelines on living.

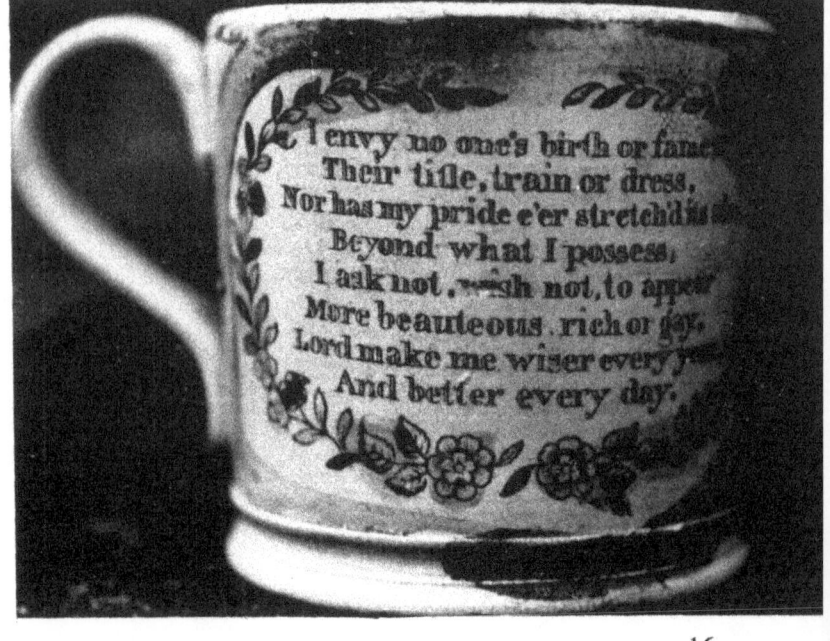

Baptist Girls' Life Brigade in 1923

This shows its members on 3rd June all smiling for the camera. Local names are Heddon, Ketley, Dovedale, Jones, West, Hillam, Wyatt, Fry, Hoskins, Olver, Hallett and Violet Dustan. The Y.M.C.A. is on the right and Mr. Henwood, baker, stables are behind the wall on the left. They were used for chapel services in 1901 before the chapel was built in 1902.

Baptist Chapel

The interior of the chapel is seen here sometime after 1902 and will bring back happy memories to the older church members who now worship in the Fletemoor Road building. The old chapel is now used as a garage.

Co-operative Women's Guild

The St. Budeaux branch of the Guild was formed on 21st March, 1904, and this shows their twenty-fifth anniversary. Mesdames Treloar, Bracewell, Hurst, Blatchford, Cock, Andrews, Redding, Smith and Councillor Clara Daymond, whose husband provided and built the adjoining Y.M.C.A. on his Tresluggan Road land. Daymond Road and Daymond House record their work in the parish. Mrs. C. Daymond was worshipful master of the Golden Hind lodge in 1933, and Mr. George Daymond was first elected to the parish council in 1902.

Programme of Music

TO BE PLAYED BY THE BAND OF THE

Plymouth Corporation : Tramways and Transport :

(By kind permission H. P. Stokes, Esq., Engineer and General Manager.)

Conductor : Mr. C. E. Lewenden (Cert. B.M.), R.A.M.

March	"Entry of the Gladiators"	*Fucik.*
Selection	"Community Land"	*Stodden.*
Descriptive	"A Hunting Scene"	*Bucalossi.*
Fox Trot	"I want to be alone with Mary Brown"	*Gilbert.*
Valse	"Midsummer"	*Marigold.*
Selection	"A Country Girl"	*Monckton.*
Fox Trot	"C.o.n.s.t.a.n.t.i.n.o.p.l.e"	*Carlton.*
Alaskan Love Song	"Cocheco"	*Reeves.*

INTERVAL

March	"Amour de Patrie"	*Tufille.*
Selection	"A Musical Jig-saw"	*Aston.*
Valse Lente	(a) "Just like Darby and Joan"	*Gilbert.*
	(b) "When you played the Organ"	*Gilbert.*
Fox Trot	(a) "Ice Cream"	*Johnson.*
	(b) "She don't Wanna"	*Ager.*
Descriptive	"In a Monastery Garden"	*Ketelby.*
Selection	"La Gran Via"	*Valverdi.*
Fox Trot	(a) "Trail of the Tamarind Tree"	*Nicholls.*
	(b) "Honolulu Song Bird"	*Stone.*

PATRONS.

Vice-Admiral Sir Rudolph W. Bentinck, K.C.B., K.C.M.G.
Major Leslie Hore-Belisha, M.P.
Rear Admiral Oliver Backhouse, C.B., Admiral Supt., Devonport.
Capt. C. W. Round Turner, C.M.G., Commodore, R.N. Barracks, Devonport
Captain C. G. Ramsey, R.N., H.M.S. Impregnable.
Capt. E. G. Robinson, V.C., O.B.E., R.N., H.M.S. Defiance, Devonport.
His Worship the Mayor of Saltash (Councillor J. A. Venn)
Major Sir Gerald Fowler Burton.   Major J. Clifford Tozer.
Engineer-Captain T. H. B. Bishop, R.N.
Samuel Gluckstein, Esq.   C. Griffiths, Esq.
W. H. Mounstephen, Esq., J.P.   J. B. Boyd Love, Esq., J.P.
W. Howett, Esq.

OFFICIALS.

President : THE MAYOR OF PLYMOUTH
(Councillor W. H. Priest, Esq.)
Vice-President : MRS. COUNCILLOR G. A. DAYMOND.
Chairman : G. A. DAYMOND, Esq., 9 Mt. Tamar Villas, St. Budeaux.
Vice-Chairmen : E. TRENCHARD, Esq., 8 Agaton Road, St. Budeaux
F. E. BATTERS, Esq.
Hon. Secretary : WALTER C. WYATT, 4 Baden Terrace, St Budeaux.
Asst. Secretary : G. L. THOMAS, Esq., 16 Sithney Street, St. Budeaux.
Hon. Treas.: JAMES WARE, Esq., The Kloof, Wolseley Rd., St Budeaux.
Committee :
Messrs. E. HOSKING, C. G. BIRCH, C. A. DAYMOND, W. BATTERS, W. LYLE, W. PEARCE, H. CIVIL, E. DUSTAN, H. DINGLE, W. RIDDELLS.

OFFICERS OF THE DAY.

Judges—
LIEUT.-COMDR. J. M. PIPER, R.N.   LIEUT.-COMDR PAYNE, R.N.
REV. RAINALD J. R. SKIPPER.
Clerks of the Course—
LIEUT.-COMDR. E. W. ROGERS, R.N.   LIEUT. J. WILKINSON, R.N.
Asst. Clerks of the Course—
A. A. SECCOMBE, Esq.   H. CIVIL, Esq.
Timekeeper—LIEUT.-COMDR. R. PURDY, R.N.
Starter—LIEUT.-COMDR. W. ST. A. MALLESTON, V.C., D.S.C., R.N.
Assistant Starter—F. E. BATTERS, Esq.
Gunman—E. G. HOSKING, Esq.

St. Budeaux Regatta

This combined with a visit to the Saltash Passage Tea Gardens was a very popular occasion and Mr. Menheneott recalls one in 1870. My father was treasurer for many years and due to failing health was unable to organise another event after 18th August, 1928. It is interesting to see the last patrons, officials, music programme and officers of the day. Many people will remember the Tramways' Band and a programme of music is shown here. Our vicar, the Rev. R. J. Skipper, took an active part in all parish events.

Baptist's Ladies Rowing Club

Here they are preparing to embark in their six-oared gig *Rowena*. Mr. Rendle, their cox and captain, carries the cast-iron kettle for the Saturday afternoon tea. Miss Violet Dustan was the club secretary for twenty-five years. The men of the church had their own boat *Young Rod* and competed in the regatta for the Harkcom Cup. These boats were Ex-Royal Navy surplus to service requirements only costing a few pounds each.

St. Boniface Boating Club

They competed in the 1928 St. Budeaux Regatta rowing in the race for St. Budeaux clubs in service pattern, six-oared, gigs. They competed against *Young Rod*, St. Budeaux Baptists, *Winning Youngster*, St. Budeaux Y.M.C.A., and *Brown Hilda*, Royal Albert Rowing Club.

St. Budeaux Carnival

This was one of the many annual events in the locality which had support from the shop keepers and business community. J. Cleave's contractors lorry provides a vantage point for Rule Britannia and her retinue. Many churches also took part in the very popular event — a relic of the horse and cart era.

Weston Mill and Kings Tamerton Engravings of 1804

These two rare illustrations show part of the localities during the first decade of the last century. The Saltash Highway Trustees turnpike house, with its gate, is on the far side of the bridge in the upper engraving. One of the six farms is in the lower illustration with a shepherd driving sheep along the old highway. Kings Tamerton was formerly known as *Tanbretone* and Weston Mill takes its name from Geoffrey de Weston.

Building of the Tamar Bridge in the 1850s

This rare picture clearly shows the hustle and bustle of the building operations for Brunel's famous bridge for his broad-gauge railway going into Cornwall. It was opened in 1859.

Views of the water tight tube, 36 feet in diameter and 95 feet long, built with an air tight chamber being sunk perpendiculary in the centre of the Tamar to construct the strong granite column to support the centre pier. Several workmen were accidentaly killed on the site and their names are recorded in the parish burial registers with Millbrook Cottage addresses.

The Spanish Armada Arsenal

Gunpowder stored at Kinterbury was used during the Armada sea battles but as this is a very sensitive area, the photograph of Drake's old wharf cannot be shown. An extract from Mr. Evan's parish records states "On 26th January, 1821, forty barrels of powder exploded killing Richard Carne, aged 62 years, and James Matthewson, aged 19 years". The War Department and Admiralty own the land previously used as a Naval Depot, Artillery Barracks, a Metropolitan Police Depot and quarters for offices and workmen. A day school was provided which was also used for a church and Sunday School. This 1894 group of scholars includes members of the Slemon family.

Bull Point Government School

This 1898 photograph shows Miss Cross, the teacher from the school, with her class at Saltash Passage. She later married a Mr. Tauranac. It is now interesting to compare this scene with the present day showing buildings still standing although many alterations above the road have taken place.

Granite Coat of Arms

I wonder how many Barne Barton Primary children have noticed this stone set in the southern end of the barn. It recalls the marriage of R. Elliot, Kinterbury, to E. Beele, Barne and has the date 1657.

Saltash Passage Building

This very old slate hung building was the former residence of Admiral Sir Peter Richards, K.C.B., Lord Commissioner of the Admiralty, who at the time commanded the *Cornwallis* and *Hibernia*. The building was acquired by Devonport Corporation in 1898 and has undergone many changes after falling into disrepair in 1914.

Donkey Stable

This dilapidated cob-walled building was demolished by the owners of the *Royal Albert Bridge Inn*. It consisted of a ground storey and upper storey which was used for church services and as a Sunday School. The ground floor was used for stabling a donkey.

An Old Parish Pump

This is probably the last remaining parish pump which has been restored and re-erected by Mr. Michael Horn at the back of his house in Normandy Way. Wells often ran dry during the summer months and water had to be obtained from the springs in Ernesettle Wood. In 1892 most of the local houses had their own well or pump.

Ernesettle Farm and Fields

These two views from the church were taken in 1914 with Agaton farmlands in the foreground. They dramatically illustrate how once well known open spaces can soon be changed into built up areas. The railway bridge below Tamerton Foliot creek can be identified in the background.

It would be an interesting exercise to draw in this area with present houses and buildings then indicate the direction of various roads built over the land.

Ernesettle Estate

This view, taken in the 1950s, records the first development of houses and factories in the Ernesettle locality. The post-war years saw a tremendous growth in buildings which have now linked up with the northward spread of the city dwellings.

Ernesettle House

Very few photographs have been taken of Ernesettle House, the homestead of the Elliotts in 1860. It is now a scheduled building and is part of the Depot complex. The Tamar Bridge road runs right below the old mansion.

The Changing Scene

Ernesettle House, farm and Newlands Cottage (demolished in 1922) were all built by Mr. W. E. Elliot in the 1860s. What would be his reaction to his valley view disappearing under the new Tamar Bridge road?

Moor Farm View in 1934

This view towards the farm was taken from the Southern Railway goods yard and shows the old tram lines in the foreground. Note the narrow Wolseley Road leading to St. Budeaux Square. The building developments had just started. Mount Tamar mansion and Kings Tamerton can be seen among the trees in the background.

Camel's Head Inn

In 1835 the Rev. C. T. Collins-Trelawny of Ham erected the inn and installed their valuable and respected servant James Rickard as the first landlord. He died there in 1856 and was succeeded by his nephew. The photograph shows the shops and the Devonport tram on its way to St. Budeaux.

The Changing Scene

This 1900 Camel's Head scene photograph shows West Ham Terrace which was later demolished to widen the road. The inn still remains a bottleneck but will go with the present large scheme of constructing the by-pass.

The Changing Scene

The lower houses in Ernesettle Lane and Higher Lea Terrace have been demolished. This postcard view includes W. Tozer's post office and was taken sometime before 1914. Some form of delivery cart is at the top of the hill.

Top of Victoria Road

It is difficult to remember the top of this road, leading to Crownhill Road, which has disappeared under the construction work for the new roundabout. The car in the foreground is heading towards the *Blue Monkey Inn* and will pass to the south of the parish church.

The Changing Scene

The cars have just passed *The Blue Monkey* inn on route to St. Budeaux Square with a last view of the school on the far hill. This has now gone and the site cleared for the new bridge road with a large roundabout in the foreground. The parish church stands in the background.

Site of School

This was the site of the St. Budeaux Foundation School which has now been excavated to build the fly-over bridge to the new by-pass. Visitors will now have no difficulty in finding Drake's Church and will receive a warm welcome from our vicar the Rev. Michael Jones.

The Henn Gennys Hatchments

The union between Captain Henn and Mary Gennys is celebrated by two hatchments said to be the finest in Devon. They can be seen above the south aisle in the parish church. As Mary Gennys was an heraldic heiress her paternal arms is placed on a small shield in the centre of the Henn arms with the mottos *Mors Janua Vitae* (Death is the Gate of Life). As the right hand is white over the left hand this shows that Edmund survived his wife Mary.

Whitleigh Hall, the Henn Gennys Homestead

The hall was sold in 1922 to pay for estate duties and it was blitzed in 1941. It had an imposing portico entrance leading to the entrance hall with a drawing room, library, lounge, smoking room and ten bedrooms. Owned by Nicholas and Christiana Docton before 1721, it came into the possession of John Gennys and then Captain Edmund Henn through marriage in 1800. There are four memorials in the church to the different families.

The second hatchment with the date 1869, with the faded motto *Deo Est Gloria* (For Gennys) with Edmund B. Henn Gennys (son of Edmund Henn Gennys) arms in black on the right side showed that his wife, Ann Chapple, survived him.

Mount Edgcumbe Industrial Training Ship, 1877 to 1920

This was moored on the Tamar and provided a home and gave training to homeless and destitute orphans. It was a well known sight in this locality for many years. In 1910 Captain H. Wesley Harkcom was appointed Captain Superintendent of the ship having succeeded a Mr. Kitt. He was a rowing expert and encouraged the young people in this activity. The upper view shows boys from the ship leading the Breakwater crew in the twelve-oar cutter *Challenge* race against the background of ships laid up after the First World War. They were Q-ships, destroyers and submarines. Members of the ship's band assemble on deck in the lower photograph. The band often gave concerts on St. Budeaux green and in the parish church.

Gypsies at Saltash Passage

They were here from 1900 to 1914 and were mainly engaged in pegmaking which they sold around the area. They were not a nuisance to local folk and fed on rabbits and hedgehogs cooked in clay. The old Southern Railway cut the springs which fed the nearby wells so Earl Compton erected a pump from which the Tamarside residents obtained their water.

St. Boniface Church

This postcard picture records part of the ceremony held on 14th May, 1913. The Bishop of Plymouth, Rural Dean and Archdeacon of Plymouth, the Lord Mayor and the vicar of St. Boniface, the Rev. H. H. Ensor, were in attendance with many other dignatories. Sergeant Wallis with Constable Bawden are in the background.

Preparation for the 1908 Regatta

Plenty of activity here on the eve of the annual regatta which was, for many years, one of the major events in the local calendar. The scene has changed somewhat and the practice of hanging out washing on a beach line has long discontinued. Note the Saltash Exchange and the national telephone pole.

St. Budeaux Foundation Church of England Junior School

Very few parishes can boast of a school which was founded as early as 1717. It was originally sited on the village green and was rebuilt on a new site in 1876. These two views record the once familiar limestone school and school house for so many years serving the educational needs of St. Budeaux children. These buildings have been demolished to make way for the new Tamar Bridge road, the construction of which is still in progress during the writing of this book. Many former pupils will view, with some nostalgia, these photographs.

Children at Play

A typical scene in any school playground with children romping around, but in this case one that will be shortly covered by a new road system. The last staff to work in the old school were Mr. Rodney Dart, headmaster, Mr. John Finch, deputy, Mrs. Weekes, Mrs. McArthur, Miss Squance, Mrs. Cook, Miss Know, Mrs. Gray, Mrs. Cairns and Mrs. Olive Dickenson, secretary.

School Governors

A proud moment for the governors is recorded here. Messrs. Yates, Warren, Fisher, Baker, Mrs. Stratton, wife of Dr. A. B. Stratton, Rev. Richard Read, chairman, Mrs. Grierson, wife of Dr. E. J. Grierson, and Commander Venning make up the group assembled in the old school. The Rev. M. D. Jones is now chairman of the governors.

The New School opened in 1981

Former pupils of the St. Budeaux Foundation Church of England Junior School, who have left the district, will be interested to see the front and side views of this excellent modern building complete with an indoor swimming pool in Priestley Avenue, Higher St. Budeaux. It was dedicated by the Rt. Rev. Eric Mercer, Lord Bishop of Exeter, on the 12th June, 1981, in the presence of the Lord Mayor of Plymouth, Councillor R. V. Morrell. Miss Phyllis Ide, a former pupil, came to the service. She was born at Budshead Mill and crossed fields to attend school winning many prizes for very good attendance.

Arthur L. Clamp – the man behind the books

Arthur Leslie Clamp was a man of boundless energy with a passion for helping others, particularly through his love of history. A printer by trade, he started his career in a printing company before moving his family from Exeter to Plymouth to teach at the Plymouth College of Art and Design, where he eventually became the Head of the Printing Department.

A Devoted Family Man

Arthur with his five children.

Despite his love of teaching, Arthur prioritised his family, always making it home by 5:30pm for tea. He and his wife, Rosemary, raised five children: Susan, Angela, Elizabeth, David, and Steven. Arthur would often combine his love of family and history by taking his children on Sunday walks, encouraging them to appreciate historical monuments by taking photos or making crayon rubbings of gravestones for his books. The family home at 203 Elburton Road was a hub of activity, with a large garden, featuring a two-storey fort and a makeshift swimming pool.

A Lifelong Learner and Adventurer

Arthur's thirst for knowledge extended beyond history to a deep curiosity about the world. He was passionate about exploring different cultures, traditions, and cuisines, often taking advantage of his long summer holidays as a teacher to travel to places like India, Russia, South America, the middle east and the USA, sometimes bringing one of his children along. This adventurous spirit even influenced his home life, as seen by the short-lived family tradition of steam-cooking vegetables after a trip to Iceland.

History is a prominent feature of family days out

Community and Philanthropic Spirit

His commitment to serving others was evident in his long-standing involvement with the Elburton Methodist Church. He was the Sunday School Superintendent for over 15 years and served as the editor of the wider church's monthly newsletter, "The Link," for a similar duration. After Rosemary's very sad passing, Arthur later remarried and, following a chance encounter with a professor from India, established a connection with a missionary school in Chennai. Together with his new wife, Christine, he co-founded a "Sponsor a Child's Education" program that continues to this day.

Pictured left – The cover of 'The Link' complete with hand drawn sketches of each church by Angela
Below right – Arthur Clamp promoting his latest book
Below left – Arthur at home with his first wife, Rosemary
Below centre – Arthur on holiday with his second wife, Christine

A Legacy of Learning and Positivity

Arthur's greatest passion was history, which he brought to life through tireless research, documentation, and the many books he authored. He was driven by a need to "never be stuck in a rut," constantly seeking new experiences, meeting new people, and expanding his knowledge. With a positive attitude and a great sense of humour, he was always ready to help others, leaving a lasting impact on his family and community. His children, Susan, Angela, Elizabeth, David, and Steven, remember him with love and gratitude.

David Clamp, 2025

A Legacy of Local History

Below is the story of how Arthur L Clamp began writing books, in his own words, drafted shortly before he passed away in 2001. I have only made minor alterations to this text, correcting grammatical errors that he did not survive to correct himself. When I first discovered this text, I was shocked to see my name mentioned. It seems that, unbeknownst to me, I shared my first PC with him. I suspect he used it during the day when I was at school, although I do have one memory of sitting with him and showing him how it worked. It has been a pleasure to pick up where he left off and see his books republished and redistributed, and to know that I was part of the story, even back then. It was also fascinating to discover that his pricing structure matches the way I have tried to price the books, with a third going to local sellers and the rest covering printing costs with a little left over for my expenses.

I am his eldest grandson, and it is a privilege to curate his legacy, which we are calling 'The Clamp Collection'. The very last line of the text originally reads "The following pages list all the titles." Sadly, that page is missing and we have no record of all the books he published and knowing that some of those were researched by other authors makes the process of finding them even harder. I look forward to one day completing the collection and seeing them all available again. And maybe, one day, I'll even start writing my own to add to the series. For now, here is his story in his own words.

Steven Gibson, 2025

Writing and Publishing Booklets on Local Topics and Areas

I started this interest in either 1968 or 1969 when living in Woodford. I had by these dates established the Department of Printing and I think I must have been looking for something different to do. The first titles were of A5 size proofed from type set at Clarke, Doble and Brendon, Ltd., Plymouth printers, and then made up into pages and printed at Sawtell and Neilson, Ltd., Totnes.

Then began a slow process of getting them out to shops, etc. which proved to be more time consuming and difficult than actually researching, writing and getting the books into print. However, I persisted and opened a business account with Barclays Bank on the Broadway. I was advised to give it a title so I called it "Westway Publications". There came along another problem, one of storage of paper and finished books which was solved when the family moved to Elburton in 1970.

I changed the printer to Penwell, Ltd., Callington, Cornwall, as he was then just setting up himself and his prices seemed very reasonable. I did not get any of the printers to make up the complete books. I hand folded the flat printed sheets, stitched the books on a small manual table stitcher and trimmed them in a small hand turned guillotine which I bought from someone in Penzance for £40. It was brought up in a van.

The trouble and time going to and fro to Callington was too much so I transferred the printing to PDS Printers, Prince Rock, Plymouth, and I have been with them ever since. Now they are at Plympton which is easy to reach and they fold the flat sheets which was turning out to be a long chore which only saved a small part of the printing costs.

All my first titles were written by myself. I took the photographs and developed them in the loft of the house, the type was set by now on a computer situated in the house at Elburton from which I had collected photographic lengths of text to cut up and law down as pages.

At some point I decided that I would do my own film processing of lith film so I bought a large second hand process camera from Kingsbridge and learnt through trial and error to make line negatives of the text and halftone negatives of the illustrations which proved more difficult than I anticipated. The main problem was trying to keep the developer in the large dish at the correct temperature as any change would affect the developing time. I replaced this old camera with a brand new one bought from Croydon, Surrey, costing £900. This has turned out to be a great asset cutting out an expensive part of the printer's costs and one crucial aspect of the work which I could control.

By the middle 1970s there were many outlets I had contacted in Plymouth, up to Dartmoor, Exeter, around to Torbay, Totnes, Dartmouth and the South Hams. The market for local books was much greater than I had first thought and through getting to know many local people undertaking research themselves had the chance to help and make up books for other people who had in most instances, got together a collection of photographs with some text in a rather muddled way. Through my experience in print I was able to shape up their work and get it into print and in every case I had to pay the printer and let the person have the royalties. In the majority of titles produced in this manner this was another way of producing titles and it did give some profit to my work. However, I must say that in a few cases I lost out by either the other person getting the numbers wrong, not returning any monies from stock I delivered or they thought that more of their books should have been sold.

The print run was usually 1,000 copies and from time to time I have had reprints of 250 copies. It took about ten years to clear the first print run so I always had large stocks in the garage, workshop, etc. The numbers sold during the early years was about 7,000 copies a year increasing to around 9,000 copies and for the whole of the enterprise about 500,000 have been sold. The booklets have become part of the local scene and many people collect them, shops regularly order copies and I go around certain areas month by month restocking or replacing titles as necessary.

During the past year or so I have started setting the text on a Packard Bell PC, something which I should have done some years back. I share it with Steven Gibson, my grandson. There appears to be no end to the market for local books, but I could not earn a regular income because of the long time it takes to sell stock.

However, now exceeding 100 titles made up mainly of A4 twenty-four page booklets, some folded guides, with selling prices set with a third going to the shop which is the trade custom, the original idea has been quite successful and could go on for ever.

Apart from monetary benefits, however spasmodically these might be, I have learnt a lot myself, met many interesting people and have become part of the local scene with requests to give talks and to advise people about getting into print.

Arthur L Clamp, 2001

This newspaper article, published by the Evening Herald on 17th August 2001, forms a good record of his life. Just as he encourages us to learn more about local history, we encourage you to learn a little about him. For that reason, we have included these pages at the back of all the most recently republished books, in honour of his memory and recognition of his contribution to the community.

www.ingramcontent.com/pod-product-compliance
Lightning Source LLC
Chambersburg PA
CBHW061405070526
44584CB00031B/4167